Team Oriented P

How to brainstorm to fina uii... process root cause and the system root cause

Table of Contents

Chapter		**Page**

Appendices

Preface

My prior book 8D Team Based Problem Solving – an Instructive Example, was published in April 2013 and has had modest sales. I believe so strongly that the "Instructive Example" is an important concept that I included it as an appendix in this book.

The first book was intended to be an example for problem solving teams in which they could see all of the elements of a good problem solving effort and use it as a template in their own efforts. This would give them the benefit of making sure that all of the elements of problem solving were considered by their teams. The idea in the first book was based my experience that virtually all of the problems solving summaries (i.e. 8D's) are very flawed. Without indulging in hyperbole, I estimate that only two or three percent of problem solving exercises are rigorous or even serious efforts. My hope for the first book was that managers or serious individuals could start a wave which turned around this acceptance of gravely inadequate efforts in order to satisfy a system for "a piece of paper" called an 8D. Also, I think managers who really want to solve problems could use this initial book to evaluate problem solving efforts and provide meaningful feedback. Properly done, this could effect a change within the organization by coaching internal and external groups in their problem solving efforts.

During my long career I could never fathom why organizations did not focus directly on problem solving.

The biggest unsolved riddle that I carry away from my career is centered on the lack of focus paid by organizations toward problem solving. Every good supervisor, manager, executive knows this fact:

> *"If we could manage our business such that all major problems were attacked <u>like our future depended on it</u>[2], we would cut our costs beyond belief and we would gain a competitive edge which would position our organization for a better future."*

The mystery to me has always been and remains:

> *"Why, then, do we accept woefully inadequate problem solving efforts and it's inevitable high total cost to the system."*

Problem solving efforts are obviously needed when a major issue arises such as a customer rejection or a field problem. A well-run organization also looks at its internal issues on a regular basis. These companies know the total cost of each problem and they have regular team actions to work on the top problems. When problems are resolved with verification, the next highest group of problems is set upon by the team.

---

[2] This **is** true – the organization's future does depend upon on solving problems

About the cover

I chose the cover photo because it seemed appropriate for this book. It is an old commercial sign painted on a brick wall. I took this photograph while on vacation in Savannah, Georgia in 2009. The brick building is interesting and the signage in this picture includes two businesses of past glory:

American Specialty & Import Co.

GE Industrial Electric Refrigerators

I assume both of these business enterprises are now, like the sign, only faded memories. I tried to look up the history of these companies, but found nothing of significance. (GE, of course is one of the most successful businesses in the world[3], but I could not find a reference to Industrial Electric Refrigerators.) There are several other similar photos which are can be found by searching on Google Pictures. In any case, I have taken the liberty to speculate that the failure to solve problems was their downfall. You can see that the building itself has had several problems which have had superficial solutions. There are many lines in the wall in which cracks were repaired with new bricks and plaster. The partial view of the American flag is interesting and I think it represents the American spirit. Companies like this were important in the building of our economy and made the US a world economic power. Some companies survived while others have faded, but we certainly did more with our people and resources than did other world powers.

To retain that competitive edge in the new "world economy", the American businesses need to produce the best products at the lowest possible total cost[4]. To accomplish this, one big factor is solving the problems that drive customers away and add cost. The message of this book is that it is rewarding and, in fact, easy to solve problems if management fully supports problem solving.

---

[3] A large reason for GE's world competitiveness is directly attributable to Jack Welch, the CEO form 1981 to 2000. Mr. Welch adopted the 6-sigma program across all of GE in 1995 (http://en.wikipedia.org/wiki/Jack_Welch). This program is, among other things, a systematic method to find root causes of problems and implement permanent corrective actions.

[4] Total Cost represents all costs associated with production and delivery of goods and/or service. This includes the obvious costs to the customer such as warranty or repairs. It also includes the cost of safety and of damage to the environment. If a company pollutes the air, water, or earth anywhere in the product cycle, someone has to bear these costs. It is easy to see in the case of poor quality. If you buy a car because it was the lowest price car available, it would not be a good decision if it had a lot of expensive repairs, a short life, and a horrific safety record.

Chapter 1
Obtain management support.

The assumption is that upper management in each organization whole-heartedly supports the idea of problem solving. In fact, they typically give rewards to people who they perceive to be solving the problems of the company. I will go out on a limb here and say that 90% of upper management really pays lip service to the idea of solving problems. Once the "Fix" has been declared and the internal or external customers are apparently satisfied, the issue is considered to be behind us. When the same problem reappears, the very same team "fixes" it again, possibly with the same woefully inadequate actions as per the previous times. *(Example: How many times have your problems been fixed with the old standby, "Retrain the operators?")*

If your management expects the cause to be found and the fix to be magically implemented, it is time to enlighten your managers or else move to a different company where competitive forces demand discipline in problem solving. Solving any complex problem requires that those individuals whose activities are impacted, including those who may be outside your company if applicable, commit to a few days of focused attention on problem solving and action planning.

If you are involved in problem solving either as a team leader or a team member, stand your ground and insist that management demonstrates their commitment to resolution by providing the time and resources for a team approach. EMPHASIS: The management should kick off the team meeting by stating their support. If they are too busy or feel that "It should be obvious" that they support the effort, it is a red flag which can doom the effort if management is not willing to give open, unqualified support for solving the problem.

Management support should clearly include stating support for finding the potential root causes, establishing plans to determine the true root causes, and developing action plans for both process root causes and system root causes. In addition, management should clearly be willing to allocate both the time and resources necessary for the problem solving team to accomplish its goals.

In order to be clear, this book will use the following definitions:

1. Team: A group of people who have a stake in problem resolution. They must have either direct power to implement a solution or the direct support of management toward that end. Of course this is based upon management's acceptance of the team's analysis that their measures are cost effective.

2. Cost effective: The expenditure to implement the recommended actions are proven (sometimes they may have to be estimated) to have a reasonable payout as a result of problem elimination. An effective manager would not generally endorse a solution that does not reduce expense unless the added cost is due to the protection of the environment or reduction of worker liability. Note: Cost in this context is the Total cost of

the system. This includes costs to customers, suppliers, and to the environment. Proposals which would prevent pollution, illness or injury are justified by upper management because of their impact on society.

3. Process Root Cause: This includes the universal definition of "process." It can include office procedures or lack thereof; it can include financial rules, marketing approach, internal methods, etc, etc. etc. The best definition of Process Root Cause is the immediate reason the problem occurred. In a manufacturing operation, examples might be "The wrong cutting tool was used," or "the injection molding cycle was altered, as a few examples. In an office environment, it could be as simple as "The order number was not legible" or, "The customers are dropping us because of our failure to provide volume discounts."

4. System Root Cause: In the long run, this is the most important concept. It is also the most overlooked area. If your organization has repeat problems, this area was overlooked. The system root cause can best be characterized by asking the questions:

- What allowed this to happen in the first place?

- Why did the problem, once it existed, escape our detection?

- What in our organization would have to be changed to ensure the problem can never happen again?

To elaborate with a manufacturing example, suppose that a fabricated part was sent to the customer with a part missing. In this case, the team found the root cause to be a missing welding operation. Ok, so they found the welding operation needed maintenance and "Fixed" the problem and started making good parts again. What system issue caused the process problem? One view would be to say that the maintenance system waits until bad parts are generated before it performs its maintenance duty. An inviolable rule is *"if you make bad parts, some will get mixed into the accepted parts."* In this case, it would be recommended that the maintenance department implement a Preventive Maintenance (PM) program and all areas which need periodic maintenance be identified with maintenance intervals. This sounds good and it is, however it is not enough. The maintenance records should be recorded with monthly summaries. If we find that the chosen maintenance cycle is not effective we should alter it. In this view, the maintenance department now has a management metric which they should review monthly. Their PM frequencies and database should become a living document which is modified as they encounter new information.

Another example of a system root cause would be the case where a product was fully designed and tested with successful results. Then a change in the product resulted from the implementation of an idea on a cost savings program. In the cost savings project, there was awareness of the need for corrosion durability of the new design, so it was given a 24 hour corrosion test and passed. Later, the cost reduced product had field failures due to corrosion. As it turned out the new coating was not as robust to the handling and damage incurred by final assembly and small nicks and scratches became initiation sites for corrosion. This was not seen in the test because the part was tested as a sub-assembly without going through the entire process of final assembly. The corrective action in this case would be to establish engineering requirements for testing of product changes. Specifically parts to be tested for corrosion must be exposed to the entire assembly process. The engineering requirements would then become a living document which would be modified each time more knowledge was brought into the system. A more stringent fix would be to prohibit any non-essential changes to a product once it is released. This seems severe, but it takes only one big mistake to wipe out a lot of cost savings.

As an example outside of manufacturing, we can consider a case where customers were given inappropriate billing charges. The initial review found that firm quotes were prepared by the sales department with input from several other departments. When the actual work was completed, the costs were collected and reviewed to see if they were in-line with the company's mark-up. If they were not in-line, the price could be changed from the quoted price providing that the customer agreed to the higher price in writing. The Sales Department had the job of documenting the agreement. For multiple reasons, this documentation was lost and the billing department began to rely on a verbal direction from Sales. The fix in this case could be to ban verbal directions for these costs and provide the sales force with wireless Smart Tablets which connect to the company's mainframe computer. The Sales person could pull down a form and get the customer's signature on the spot. There would be no need for matching paper agreements to the original quote. All billing information could be on one electronic file.

Chapter 2
Use the team approach (environment)

Upper management should openly commit to supporting the team. This is most important and is discussed in the previous chapter.

Management should choose the team leader. See the next chapter for recommendations in this case. The team leader should have input into the make up of the team. As an example, if a person who is habitually inattentive, negative or disruptive is suggested, he/she may be ruled out if it is in the best interest of team dynamics. In some cases, however, disruptive individuals can turn out to be the highest contributors if you can find out why they are behaving in that manner and then harness their energy toward the team goals.

A conference room must be set aside for the problem solving team. It is very important to remove the individuals from the environment of their day-to-day job. This could be on-site but an off-site conference room is highly recommended for this important task. Participants must have management support to ensure that someone can fill in their duties and protect them from receiving text messages and cell phone calls. The facilitator must emphasize the no calls or texts rule at the start of the meetings. Mid-morning and mid-afternoon breaks are the time to deal with these types of communications. Distractions will diminish the team effort.

Each department within the organization as well as outside areas which interact with the organization should be considered for having a team member in the meeting. Those areas which have a significant stake in the problem should have a representative at the meeting. In my experience, problem solving teams are usually small (6 to 8 people) but they can be large in complex problems (18-20). Let's use a hypothetical example to illustrate a team which needs some great depth.

Hypothetical problem: A critical plastic gear fails in operational use. In this case the part is purchased as a component and assembled into a gearbox which is furnished to an original equipment manufacturer for inclusion in a refrigerator icemaker. Preliminary potential root causes are as follows:

a) Improper molding resin

b) Improper molding conditions

c) Damage during assembly onto gear shaft

d) Chemical attack from lubrication oil in the gearbox

e) Assembly damage from the manufacturing operation at the refrigerator manufacturing plant

f) The refrigerator icemaker design has changed and it is now loaded more than the original design intent of the gear.

g) Handling, shipping and storage through all phases, including the associated temperature and humidity effects.

h) In both the gearbox manufacturing operation and the customer's refrigerator manufacturing operation, the process should be carefully evaluated for repair loops, requalification of rejects, customer returns, and any other loop which could put gears or gearboxes back into the system after initial assembly.

In the case above, how does anyone get all of the information needed to understand the problem, much less resolve it? The answer is that an *individual* is very unlikely to solve this problem. A team approach would look at each potential root cause and include a knowledgeable team member for each area of concern (a) through (g) above.

a) The material source expert may be the best team member to evaluate the adequacy of the molding resin.

b) Similarly the material source expert or a manufacturing engineer would be a good team member to evaluate the molding conditions.

c) A Manufacturing expert as well as a Manufacturing Engineering expert could best determine if the assembly onto the gear shaft could be a contributor.

d) Material experts, possibly from the material source could advise on the particular resin and its potential deterioration from the lubricating oil.

e) The customer (Refrigerator Plant Manufacturing Engineer) could work with the team to review the process of assembly and its potential to damage the gear.

f) The customer (Refrigerator Plant Design Engineer) can review the design change and its added load on the gear.

g) All Phases should evaluate their shipping, handling and storage as potential contributors to gear failure. This information could be given to the manufacturing engineer to bring to the team meeting.

h) Manufacturing loops of any kind are dangerous sources of problems. This should include (in this case) both the organization with the problem as well as the customer organization.

This last item, manufacturing loops, is important enough to have a little more discussion. The examples are numerous but let me illustrate with an example of a repair loop. When the gearbox is manufactured, it is tested at the end of the line to see if it is ok to pack and ship. This testing involves many parameters. All failures are tossed or dropped into a reject bin. Later, at a slack time, an operator is given the task of either simply retesting the unit, repairing it, or else he may be instructed to disassemble it and save the good parts for future production. In this example, at least four negative things could happen (in reality there are many more bad things that could happen).

1. The plastic gear develops a hairline crack from the drop into the repair bin.

2. Simply retesting the unit is an example of "Manufacturing Roulette." If this is the case in your operation there is a need to discourage this behavior in the strongest terms possible. This actually points to the need to make sure the tester's decision making ability meets the intended goal and the testers are set up equally. The author has personally seen the case where there were three testers at the end of the line and all rejects were retested through tester #3 which had the highest acceptance rate of the three testers.

3. The person doing the retest and/or repair may be different each time, so there is no consistency to their method. In addition, off line operations are generally not watched closely so a person with poor

training or poor attitude can do pretty much what he/she wants.

4. Disassembly is usually done with hand tools and by operators who are not fully trained or aware of the potential to damage parts. As parts are removed and inspected, they are put in "Good" or "Rejected" boxes for return to assembly. Such a system is a wide-open door for mixing of rejected parts with good parts.

Chapter 3
The team leader

The team leader needs to be someone who is comfortable with the dynamics of many personality types and disciplines. He/she must listen to someone but be strong enough to stop unnecessary discussion without unnecessarily alienating individuals. This is a learned ability but some individuals seem to have a natural leadership in this respect. In mature organizations, there usually are several people who can serve as the team leader. In some organizations, this role can not be filled internally and outside resources may be needed. In these cases, the most likely internal candidates should be participating to learn from the outside resource person.

The team leader must be assigned by upper management. This gives the participants a clear signal of who has been given leadership in this role and if potential conflicts in power may exist, this action by management serves to minimize any dysfunctional behavior in this area.

As a team leader, this individual is responsible for securing a conference room with flip charts, markers, and tape or pins to secure completed flip chart sheets to the walls where the team can refer to them. Additionally, the team leader should have an agenda (see crib notes for an example) and provide breaks, refreshments, paper, pencils, etc. as needed to complete the team tasks. Finally, the team leader must have the self-confidence to direct the team and discourage any discussions which are irrelevant or personal discussions, either not related or else not open to the entire team. A good team leader will state these working rules at the beginning of the team meeting.

It is the author's opinion, based upon years of practice, that good old-fashioned paper flip charts are the best media to use in brainstorming efforts. The leader simply writes the information on the paper in large legible printing. The information is written in real time so all team members can see it. The leader checks after it is written down to see if the written words correctly convey the thought that has been stated. When the flip chart page is full, it is torn off and taped to a blank wall. If added information is put on subsequent flip chart pages, these pages are taped along side the first sheet. Once brainstorming is complete (Chapter 5,) it is best to create a Word file summary of the flip charts. This can best achieved with minimal team interruption if it is done during a break in the session.

Chapter 4
Avoid "Groupthink"

Groupthink is a dysfunctional interaction within a group which can lead to disastrous results. Typically there is fear among group members that they will not conform to upper management's wishes or else they are afraid they will embarrass themselves with an unpopular stand. There are many examples in history where people went along with an unpopular course of action because of such fears. The items below have been cited as examples of groupthink:

- Historians have pointed to the decision of Nazi Germany to invade Russia.

- The failure to anticipate the attack on Pearl Harbor

- Vietnam War

- The Bay of Pigs

(ref: http://en.wikipedia.org/wiki/Groupthink)

In recognition of the corrosive effects of groupthink, it is well worth your while to take steps to discuss this phenomenon with your team. I can't provide the reference, but I once saw a discussion by someone who interviewed President John F. Kennedy's top advisors after the decision to invade the Bay of Pigs. The first interviewee to respond after the proposal was made to invade said words to the effect (paraphrasing), *"I thought it was a terrible idea but I was the first to speak. I was afraid that saying what I think would be a direct slap in the President's face. I said that I agreed and sat back to see what the others thought."* The next person then said during the interview words to the effect *"Wow! He just agreed to that ill-advised plan, what am I missing? I was afraid to be the first to say no to this, so I agreed."* And so it went through all of the advisors. It was unanimously decided that we should invade the Bay of Pigs.

This is worth repeating. Management must directly state that all ideas are to be given. Acknowledge the dangers of groupthink and assure the group that their unfiltered input is valuable. Powerful people are often judgmental and dismissive of other's ideas and this should be discouraged. If it shows up during the group session, it must be directly addressed and stopped. This is best handled with humor which will minimize the embarrassment of everyone involved.

Many organizations have supervisors, managers, or other executives who are known for their "Top-Down" communication style. Some use intimidation and embarrassment to show their power. These people must be dealt with directly. Some can change their behavior because they are smart enough to know the detrimental impact of this management style. The top management in the organization must recognize this need and absolutely prevent this management style from poisoning such efforts. If this cannot be accomplished, then the organization must be resigned to the status quo.

Chapter 5
Brainstorming

During the brainstorming phase, the team leader has to keep things moving with minimal distraction. It is okay to let some conversations continue for a short while, it is still necessary to guide diverging conversations back to the central goal. There are many approaches to brainstorming and the following has been most successful for the author:

1. Introduction of the team members. Each person tells who they are and what their responsibilities and areas of expertise are.

2. Explain the rules of brainstorming to the group.

    Rule #1: Everyone participates (It is ok to "Pass.")

    Rule #2: No criticism is allowed *(Note – there is a method discussed later to prioritize ideas for value)*

    Rule #3: Be free to say what you feel.

3. Have each team member write down his/her idea of exactly what the problem is. This should take only 5 minutes. Once these are written down, query them in order and write their idea on a flip chart. You will find many different perceptions of what the problem description is[1] . This is the 8D step titled <u>Define the Problem</u>. In order to have an effective problem resolution, you have to have everyone working on the same problem.

4. Once you have all of these problem descriptions written on a flip chart, go back to the first person and ask them why they feel the problem is best described as they stated. Ask the team for a short "Yay or Nay" with a few minutes discussion as necessary. If someone gets into a prolonged discussion, ask them to hold off until we get to them in the seating order.

5. After you get through all the team members, ask for an open discussion on what the team should accept as the statement of the problem. The team leader's job at this point is to get a consensus problem statement. This consensus statement of the problem should be written down on a flip chart and attached to the wall for all team members to view.

[1] Each team member views the problem from a slightly different perspective. This is analogous to the fable of the 3 blind men touching an elephant. One touched the trunk and thought it was like a snake; one touched the leg and felt it was like a tree trunk, and the third touched the tail and thought it was like a straw fan swinging back and forth.

The initial step of achieving a unified problem statement may result in much discussion with many cross-outs and re-writes, but it should end up with consensus. If it is difficult to get to consensus, ask the minority view-holders why the have their particular view. If they strongly support a different view, integrate it onto the main problem statement and again try for consensus. This step is very important because if we do not agree on what the problem is, we have lost our way. We can not get to the root cause and we can not fix the problem

Chapter 6
Work on the obvious first:
The "Process Root Cause."
Why did it happen?

As soon as a problem becomes serious enough that upper management develops a concern about it, there most likely are many pockets within the organization that have knowledge of the problem. This may be a production line worker who noticed some problem or alteration and was concerned about it but found his/her concern fell on deaf ears. It could be a production repair person. It also could be a Marketing or Sales representative who had a vague complaint from the customer but neither the customer nor the representative felt it warranted further investigation. This is human nature. Some people do not recognize red flags because their inputs are not sought or their organizational placement provides "blinders" for things that do not directly affect them. Others see things that are not reported because they do not have a sense of ownership of their job. There may be other flags that point to the problem such as customer complaints, warranty, increased costs, etc. The major point here is that once a problem is known, there is a lot of potential to gather data which will get the organization on a path to dealing with the root cause in an expeditious manner.

This is where true brainstorming comes into play. In this phase we develop **potential** root causes. Actual root causes will be developed later. It can get a little wild but the team leader's job at this point should be to make sure that everyone is heard and there is no criticism. Criticism can be direct (*"That's a dumb idea!"*) or it can be a little more subtle (*"We tried that before and it did not work."* or, *"Are you kidding me?"*) In my experiences, it is best to tell the group at this phase that if someone wanted to suggest the potential root cause was the phase of the moon, that is ok. This usually brought out a few laughs or groans, but it set the stage so people were at ease to come up with ideas free of peer pressure.

Chapter 7
The next effort:
The "System Root Cause."
What **system** *failure allowed it to happen?*

System Root Causes are developed and prioritized in the same manner as are Process root causes in the previous chapter. This phase is very important and often overlooked. If an organization does not correct System Root Causes, they will suffer from repeat occurrences of the same issue.

The concept of "System Root Cause" can not be over emphasized. It often is easy to fix the process root cause because at times it is obvious. For example, something was dropped, some step was missed, the wrong material was used, an office procedure was unwritten, data was lost, etc., Merely fixing the obvious, in most cases does not prevent a recurrence of the problem. The team has to ask the question: *"What changes do we have to make so that we can eliminate the conditions which led to the process root cause?"*

In a simple example, let us consider a manufacturing example in which the customer received a machined part which was defective because it had a missing operation.

A. Process Root Cause view:

The process investigation revealed that this happened due to a broken drill bit and the automated drilling operation went through its cycle without performing the operation. The corrective actions were (a) replace the drill bit, and (b) give the operator a gage to put each part on and detect that all drilled holes were present and in the right location.

B. System Root Cause View:

The team pondered the question, *"What system conditions lead to this defect in the first place?"* In this case, with the focus on System Root Cause, the team brainstorming effort resulted in the following corrective actions: (a) Modify PM program to change drill bits on a basis that is shown by data to be free of breakage due to wear. (b) Use process parameters (vision or force sensing) to sense breakage and shut down the operation when a drill breaks.

If only the corrective actions in the process root cause view were implemented, we would have continuing problems because drill wear, work pieces can be improperly placed in the fixture, set-up can be wrong, plus many other possibilities. Additionally, our fix added a permanent cost because the operator now has to place each part on a fixture, make a judgment and then move the part to its proper location.

The System Root Cause, in this example, has an initial up-front cost to design and implement a vision system, for example. Once that cost is understood, the organization can make a business case to justify the cost based on lowering downtime, defects and rework. Additionally, they could increase productivity because we do not tie up the operator or an inspector for 100% inspection. Finally, we would eliminate costs associated with customer rejections, the need to contain and certify defective stock, go to meetings to explain our problem solving effort and numerous communications during the ongoing investigation.

In an effort to ensure we do not overlook this step, please use the forms in the <u>appendix A</u> as a guide to the team based problem solving sessions.

Chapter 8
Methodology to look at potential root causes.

Development of Potential *PROCESS* Root Causes
(See definition of process root cause in chapter 1)

Initially, go around the table and ask the first person to suggest a potential process root cause. Write it down on the flip chart and ask if you captured his/her idea adequately. Go to the next team members in succession. If someone wants to pass, that is ok and within the "everyone participates" rule.

When you get more passes than new ideas, ask the group for open discussion on potential process root causes. When someone tosses out an idea, ask them to give you time to write it down and verify that the written words capture his/her idea. When the open ideas session slows down, stop the brainstorming and tell the group if someone has a major item they want to add, they can do it later as long as it is in the team setting.

It is worth re-stating that any idea is ok. You will see that the value ideas surface during the prioritization step in the next chapter. If possible, encourage wild and crazy ideas as they tend to stimulate more imaginative contributions and this definitely breaks down barriers for timid people or those who worry that they will say something that will embarrass them.

As a side note, I once was working in England with a group of fuel system engineers on a fuel system design issue. One of the problems was associated with "Current Draw" or how much of the battery and/or generated power the fuel pump would use. One engineer suggested that the power source could be the fuel itself and there was no need for electrical circuitry to the pump. This was such a novel idea that I remember it clearly 30 years later. This engineer was a good engineer and he knew intuitively that this would not be a practical path to follow, but nevertheless, he threw out the idea. This suggestion started renewed imaginative thinking and a very good outcome resulted.

Chapter 9
Prioritizing potential root causes.

Establishing Priorities on the list of Potential
PROCESS Root Causes

A lot of people involved with problem solving are
frustrated by the ever-expanding list of possibilities to
pursue. This is especially true when a team is involved.
The answer to this fear of an impossibly large list is
easily and efficiently answered. The answer is
surprisingly simple. The team meeting contains all of the
people who not only are familiar with the concern, but
they tend to be the subject matter experts in their
individual fields. With this assemblage of experts, all of
the potential root causes can be quickly assigned
priorities by the method listed below. This method was
created by necessity and it will achieve consensus on the
priorities 100% of the time. This method is fast and
does not overlook the lower priority items. It merely puts
these lower items on a list to pursue if the team decides
to do so.

With all of the potential root causes visible to the
team on the flip chart sheets, ask each team member to
review them carefully and decide on the top 5 potential
root causes individually. Ask each team member to
decide which of the potential root causes could be a
major contributor to the problem as stated in the *team
developed Problem Statement*. (*See chapter 5*) Each team
member is to write these down on a sheet of paper giving
their personal top priority item the #5, the next priority

item #4 and so on until they complete their 5th priority with #1.

The leader should then go to the flip charts and query each team member by seating order. When the team member states that a certain potential root cause is his/her top priority, write the number 5 by the right side of that potential root cause on the flip chart. Similarly record the 2nd priority, with a number 4 and so on through his/her top 5 items. Repeat this process for all team members. You will then have multiple "scores" for several items on the flip chart. Add up the scores for each item and record the sum for each potential root cause at its left. At this point, generate a prioritized list of potential root causes with the highest number first on down to the lowest number. This can generate many potential root causes.

As a group, review the prioritized list. Using open discussion, suggest approximately 5 of the top scored items as the first priority for the team to work on.

Note: The number of 5 is an arbitrary number and it usually works well. If the leader or the team chooses another number, say 7, then the procedure would be the same. The highest priority item in this case would be assigned a score of 7.

Chapter 10
Working on the highest priority root cause:
Testing for the true root cause.

Development of a plan to test potential root causes

On a new flip chart, write the 5 top potential root causes, in priority order. In this step, we will make a simple paper spreadsheet with 5 rows (1 for each potential root cause) and 5 columns.

The columns are as follows:

1. Potential Root Cause

2. Person Responsible *(usually the subject matter expert)*

3. Suggested test to prove/disprove the potential root cause

4. Planned completion date

5. Results of test

6. Estimated % contribution to Process Root Cause
   (Sometimes this has to be a value judgment)

As a team, discuss the first Potential Process Root Cause. Ask for a volunteer to be the champion of that specific root cause. If it is obvious who should be the champion (i.e. perhaps the Manufacturing Engineer), you can say directly to him/her, "Would you agree to be the champion of this item?" Next ask him/her to suggest, possibly with team involvement, a test which would prove or disprove this specific item as a potential root cause. There are many things that can be done to help define this association with the root cause. One way would be to look at data from the manufacturing operation. How much scrap do they generate and where is it generated. Is there a maintenance item that is suggested when this issue appears? Does data exist before and after the maintenance? If not can it be generated? And so on. Each item must have a champion assigned and a plan generated to determine the relationship between the suggested root cause and the actual problem. All actions are to have completion dates and the dates must be high priority because we have management commitment to resolve the issue. Once the actions are complete, the team reconvenes and reviews each test and if there is agreement in the adequacy of the tests, the team then will have a list of actual root causes. (Some potential root causes will be proven as not associated with the concern). Then the team moves on to assess the percent each proven root cause contributes to the overall problem. Many times there are interactions where 2 or 3 or even more root causes must combine to make the problem happen.

> Example 1: Both improper molding machine parameters as well as exposure to low temperatures could contribute to unpredictable breakage of plastic parts

Example 2:   A sales department must have chronic failure to turn in customer agreed job additions as well as the billing department to rely upon verbal input from the sales force to miss-bill a customer.

Chapter 11
Action plans to eliminate or neutralize true root causes.

Development of Potential *SYSTEM* Root Causes
(See definition of SYSTEM root cause in chapter 1)

System Root Causes are developed and prioritized in the same manner as are Process root causes in the previous chapter. This phase is very important and often overlooked. If an organization does not correct System Root Causes, they will suffer from repeat occurrences of the same issue.

Chapter 12
Verification of Effectiveness of the corrective actions

Once the team implements an action aimed at eliminating the root cause, the action plan must contain an evaluation of the process to determine the effectiveness of the corrective actions. This is a dual stage determination as follows:

1. Short Term: During the initial implementation of the corrective actions, each action should be tested to see if it can reliably do what the team thought it should do. One of the ways to do this in a manufacturing process is to present the known conditions which led to the process root cause and see if the new robust process can either detect it reliably or eliminate it. With non-manufacturing concerns, a similar plan must be developed to ensure the effectiveness of the fix.

2. Long term: This usually involves data collection and a monthly summary to be reviewed by the management. This step is usually achievable using readily available data such as (in the case of manufacturing) analysis of tester rejects, inspector reports, etc. It could also be expanded to include a view of customer rejections and warranty; however ***there is a big caution here: Use of customer data or warranty data is not a main source of data for verification.*** This is too late. It should be included along with data within your control as evidence of long-term satisfaction that we have truly eliminated the problem and not just masked it from our internal view.

With non-manufacturing problem analyses, there are similar tests that must be used to verify the effectiveness. With engineering issues, there are ES tests or special tests of durability, vibration, environment, etc. With Sales, Marketing, Purchasing, MP&L, and etc. similar tests have to be designed which essentially evaluate the system for preventing or at least catching concerns before they impact the organization.

Chapter 13
Crib Notes

The following is a checklist outline to be used by a Team Leader, or Facilitator to ensure the team has covered all the steps necessary for successful problem solving.

☐ Obtain management support.
- ☐ Resources – Room, flip charts, markers etc.
- ☐ Empower the Team Leader
- ☐ Empower or solicit support of inside/outside stakeholders

☐ Use the team approach (environment.)
- ☐ All areas directly needed for resolution
- ☐ Subject matter experts

☐ The team leader.
- ☐ Provide "rules," direction and resources to the team.

☐ Avoid "Groupthink."
- ☐ Eliminate fear & promote open discussion

☐ Brainstorming.
- ☐ Everyone contributes
- ☐ No Criticism

☐ Work on the obvious first: The "Process Root Cause." Why did it happen?
- ☐ Prioritize all of the potential root causes
- ☐ Get existing data pertinent to concern
- ☐ Assign team leaders to generate new data as needed
- ☐ Generate an action plan for each priority potential root cause. Assign individuals with due dates.

Crib Notes, continued

☐ The next effort: The "System Root Cause." What system failure allowed it to happen?
  - ☐ Prioritize all of the potential root causes
  - ☐ Get existing data pertinent to concern
  - ☐ Assign team leaders to generate new data as needed
  - ☐ Generate an action plan for each priority potential root cause. Assign to individuals with due dates.

☐ Methodology to look at potential root causes.
  - ☐ Everyone participates
  - ☐ Encourage wild ideas
  - ☐ When "passing" becomes common, go to open discussion

☐ Prioritizing potential root causes.
  - ☐ Each team member identifies top 5 choices.
  - ☐ Use assigned number method
  - ☐ Work on the top priority items.
  - ☐ Retain lower priority items if needed.

☐ Working on the highest priority root cause: Testing for true root cause.
  - ☐ Subject matter experts should accept assignments.
  - ☐ Due Dates

☐ Action plans to eliminate or neutralize true root causes.
  - ☐ Each priority process or system root cause must have an action plan.
  - ☐ Test each corrective action as it is implemented
  - ☐ Establish an ongoing data collection to provide ongoing verification of the effectiveness of the actions.

This page intentionally blank
for the purpose of
formatting (Pagination)
the examples following

Appendix A: 8D – An Instructive Example

Purpose of the book:

In this example we are looking at our imaginary firm named MCP Industries. MCP is a direct supplier to Strand Industries, a major OEM. Strand has experienced a quality issue with our product. The complaint is that a small gear mechanism has a rusty output pin. A rejection has been issued against MCP Industries and they have submitted a preliminary 8D based on early investigation of the issue. In this example, MCP Industries has now prepared a full 8D to give to their customer.

This example is intended to be used as a teaching tool for improvement in the elements of 8D problem solving methodology.

There are 8 disciplines in structured problem solving (Thus the term "8D.") In this book, a realistic example is given of each discipline. A section titled "Comments" follows teach example. The comments represent clarification of what is required and it also tells what is unacceptable because certain common actions actually do not contribute to problem solving. These are the "Do's and Don'ts" which are necessary to write a good problem solving report.

Problem solving teams must have a well defined leader. This is a person who will keep the team on track and encourage positive teamwork. A good leader will work his/her way through the 8D steps and ensure that each one is completed correctly.

It is highly recommended that problem solving teams have additional training on the skills used in problem solving such as SPC, Capability, Sampling, Comparison of attribute vs. variables data, measurement error, etc. Without common understanding of these topics, the team may work at cross-purposes.

The table below shows the format for the example within this book. Each of the eight disciplines is discussed in the following order:

Explanation of format for discussing the 8-disciplines

1. Identification of the discipline under discussion
2. An example of the particular step of the 8D
3. Guidance, comments and "Do's and "Don'ts

Each "Discipline" within the 8D process is discussed using a 2-section format as outlined below.

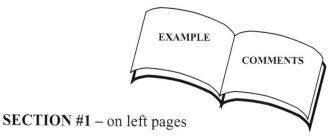

EXAMPLE

COMMENTS

SECTION #1 – on left pages

Presentation of an example which is intended to be a realistic situation. In this case, all examples are relating to a problem which was indentified by our customer. The resulting rejection of an incoming shipment was our first awareness of the issue.

SECTION #2 – on right pages

A listing of *Do's and Don'ts* for each discipline. Also included are helpful comments. This is a very important section and it is aimed at focusing on finding and correcting the root cause of the problem. Special attention is needed to prevent the team from looking making mistakes such as:

1. Erroneously listing symptoms as root causes
2. Failing to fix the root cause (i.e. adding another inspection for example).

---

3. Neglecting the need to correct the system root cause (i.e. what within the system permitted the root cause to happen and escape our detection?)
4. Seeking to blame others for the problem.

TABLE OF CONTENTS
For
An Instructive Example

Subject

1. Use the team approach

2. Describe the problem
   In customer's terms

3. Containment & short term corrective actions

4a. Define and verify root cause
   *Recognize both the System root cause
   and the Process root cause*

4b. Define and verify root cause (continued)

5. Implement and verify permanent
   corrective Actions

6. Implement and verify permanent
   corrective actions (continued)

7. Prevent Recurrence

8. Recognize the team

APPENDICES for 8D an Instructive Example

Appendix I   Fishbone Diagram

Appendix II   Is/Is-Not Analysis

Appendix III   Timeline of Events

Author's Notes   Additional discussion

#1 EXAMPLE - USE THE TEAM APPROACH

MCP Industries Personnel:

Bill Smith – Champion, Plant Manager
Don Simpson – Engineering Supervisor
Fred Russell – Receiving Inspector
Dave Brill – Grinder Operator – EI Team Leader
Mary Clark – QC Manager
George Jones – Mfg. Superintendent

Sub-Supplier Personnel:

John Brown – QC Manager, Ace Heat Treating
Bob Gardner – Tech Rep – Hi-Tek Coolants
Ann Bowen – Tech. Rep. Fab Steel Co.

Strand Industries Personnel:

Larry James - Strand Ind. Process Engineer
Bill Thompson – Product Design Engineer

#1 C O M M E N T S

CHAMPION:

He/She provides the resources and the climate for problem solving.

TEAM FORMATION:

Consider all affected activities

> Sub Suppliers of components
> Raw Material Sources
>
> Purchased services sources
>
> Customer
>
> Machine Builder
>
> Gage and/or test equipment supplier
>
> Inside/Outside experts
>
> Packaging Engineers
>
> Others

The magnitude of the problem may dictate the depth of the brainstorming phase.

Obtain the "Buy-in" of each participating activity.

GOALS – Define the 8D team goals in writing as an initial team activity. Obtain group consensus.

RULES – Clearly define the team rules.

> #1 – NO CRITICISM – Everyone's opinion is important
>
> #2 – EVERYONE CONTRIBUTES – it is ok to "pass," but each team member must participate.

#2   EXAMPLE - DESCRIBE THE PROBLEM

RUSTY OUTPUT GEAR STATIONARY PIN

On 3/17/13, The Strand Industries Main Plant rejected 17,290 pcs of output gear pins for the presence of rust. The engineering drawing requires the parts to be rust-free. A sample of 50 output gear pins revealed 17 rusty parts, or 34% defective.

#2 COMMENTS

This section must be stated in the customer's terms.

Dates must be stated – start date/end date, including production date of defects.

Frequency and percent defective must be documented

Other quantification includes:

Actual measurements and statistical capability (process potential) estimates.

State clearly what requirements exist. *This includes specifications, standards and other agreements*

5W2H: Who, What, Where, When, Why, How, How Many. It is a good practice to ask "Why" at least 5 times. *Ask "Why until it does not make sense to drill down any deeper.*

Obtain and use specifications, process flow diagrams or other schematics, which show requirements, process, inspection, travel, storage, etc.

Use minimal basic descriptions (i.e.: Rusty output gear pins) and then give a short explanatory paragraph.

Avoid the common mistake of characterizing the problem as follows:

> "The Strand Industries Main Plant found rusty output gear pins......"

The problem is that "We" made the defect, not that the customer found it.

#3 E X A M P L E – CONTAINMENT AND SHORT TERM CORRECTIVE ACTIONS

3/17/13 - All available stock was isolated and sorted with the following results:

Location	Pcs Sorted	Pcs Rejected	Percent Rejected	Confidence
Main Plant	17,290	7,123	41%	95%
Acme	96,500	8,974	9%	95%
HT Treat	38,000	1,486	4%	95%
TOTALS	151,790	17,583	12%	

3/18/13 – Sort Completion (System Purged)

Other Short Term Corrective Actions:

3/18/13 – Added 100% visual inspection at pack line – est. 95% effective.

3/18/13 – Conducted a process audit. Result – All processing parameters were judged to be acceptable to existing process standard.

3/19/13 – Reviewed all raw material in inventory for presence of (a) Undersize, (b) Excess Rust and/or pitting. NONE FOUND

3/19/13 – Reviewed the problem with the Employee Involvement group and involved the EI group in a team brainstorming activity

#3 COMMENTS

It is not necessary to know root cause at this initial time. The first objective is to protect the customer from experiencing any additional defective stock

Containment actions must extend to:

Your operations

Your warehouse

Repair/rework Area

In-transit stock: *That which is in-transit to and from customer and all sub-suppliers, platers, heat treaters, component sources, finishers, etc.*

What is the % effectiveness of your containment? How was it determined?

List any other short term actions the team has taken (These may be actions taken prior to determining root cause)

What were the dates of the containment actions?

What was found – (this should be quantified)

Audits are not acceptable as containment ACTIONS.

Key Words:

DATA
DATES
QUANTIFICATION
VERIFICATION

#4a E X A M P L E – DEFINE & VERIFY ROOT CAUSE

A Team brainstorming session of 3/17/13 resulted in identification of 3 potential process root causes and 3 potential system root causes as indicated below.

PROCESS ROOT CAUSES:

% Priority	Potential Process Root Contribution	Estimated Cause
1	New Cardboard Dunnage Separators used by Fab Metal Treating Co. have acid residue, that attacks steel.	75%
2	Coolant supplied by Hi-Tek and coolants used by Fab Metal Treating Co. do not inhibit rust.	25%
3	Stock O.D. Size from Fab Steel Co. is not sufficient to allow for "clean-up" during the rough and final grinding operations.	5%

SYSTEM ROOT CAUSES:

% Priority	Potential Process Root Contribution	Estimated Cause
1	Failure to prove-out a process change	75%

#4a C O M M E N T S

The brainstorming team should have copies of the Fishbone Diagram and the Is/Is-Not analysis on the wall for all to consider in their discussions. These two documents are very helpful in identifying potential root causes. See Appendix I and II for the Fishbone Diagram and the is/is-not analysis.

Keep asking Why, Why, Why?

As we explore each new "Why", we approach closer to the true root cause. We should stop asking "Why" when we begin to consider root causes which are clearly beyond our control (i.e.: Weather, Atmosphere, etc)

Challenge each Root Cause as a symptom or an effect.

Recognize that there is usually a PROCESS root cause and a SYSTEM root cause.

PROCESS root cause: The immediate cause, which acts directly on the manufacturing system.

SYSTEM Root cause: The underlying cause which is within the management system and permits the conditions to exist which result in the process root cause.

The team should jointly determine (or estimate) the contribution of each potential root cause. (See right-hand column in table on prior page)

A fishbone analysis should be considered MANDATORY (This is also referred to as an Ishikawa diagram). See Appendix I for an example.

Is/is-not analysis similarly should be considered MANDATORY. See Appendix II for an example.

#4b. EXAMPLE - DEFINE & VERIFY ROOT CAUSE

VERIFICATION OF ROOT CAUSE:

Cause Ident.	Estimate Date	Verification Action	% Confidence.
P-1 99+%	3/18/13	Inspection of the rust pattern on the rejected parts revealed "line" pattern of rust that indicates contact with cardboard separator surfaces	
P-2 100%	3/18/13	A lab chip test using in-process coolant developed rust on chips after 36 hours. The rust protection for this product is 48 hours with no red rust. Additionally, the coolant pH was 6.8 vs. the tech data sheet requires the pH be maintained at 7.1 to 7.3.	
P-3	3/19/13	A tolerance stack-up study indicated that minimum stock diameter when coupled with maximum finished output pin diameter, developed the potential for "no clean-up" if pitting or scale is deeper than .002"	25%

#4b C O M M E N T S – (Included in #4a comments.)

For purposes of identifying the category of root cause, the left side of the following examples has codes such as P-1, P-2, S-1, etc.   This is to highlight the categorization of the root to "Process" or to "System."   As added root causes are considered, they are numbered sequentially within each category. Also, beneath these codes there is a label such as "Prevention" or "Detection."   This is identification of the corrective actions as either working on preventing the concern or merely detecting it.   Prevention actions can significantly lower costs while Detection actions keep a lot of non-value added costs within the process.

#5/6a. EXAMPLE – IMPLEMENT AND VERIFY PERMANENT CORRECTIVE ACTIONS

VERIFICATION OF PERMANENT CORRECTIVE ACTIONS:

Cause % Ident.	Date	Corrective Actions	Estimate % Confidence
P-1 (Preve-ntion)	3/20/13	Resin coated white cardboard were reinstated in production. These are the same separators as used prior to the problem. This material has been added to the process sheets and specified on the bill of materials.	99+%
P-2 (Preve-ntion)	3/20/13	The in-process coolant will be monitored daily for pH and adjusted or discarded when it drops below pH 7.1. The PFMEA has been changed to reflect the pH controls.	99+%
P-3 (Preve-ntion)	3/24/13	All bar material was re-specified to be purchased at .003" larger stock diameter.	100%
S-1 (Preve-ntion)	3/20/13	The Fab Ht Treat Co. procedures were modified to require prove-out of all significant process changes	95%
S-2 (System)	3/26/13	The characteristic of "rust" has been added to the dock audit instruction sheet. The results will be logged in the Dock Audit record sheet	95%
S-3 (System)	4/1/13	FMEA Updated	100%

#5/6a C O M M E N T S

Label each action to identify the PROCESS or SYSTEM root cause it is acting on (This permits an "accounting" system to ensure each cause has an action directed toward it)

Identify whether each action is PREVENTION or DETECTION. (The best and lost cost solution involves the use of preventive actions)

QOS reporting systems are an excellent source of verification data.
Also use SPC charts, Cpk's, Ppk's, before and after the fix. ("...the Cpk was 0.53 prior to the fix and 1.8 after the corrective action – studies attached as back-up)
Another example: "Prior to actions, throughput losses were 1.36%. After the 3/11/13 fix, the process throughput losses were 0.04% - as per attached Percent defective (Rust) chart."

DO NOT rely on your customer for verification ! (i.e.: Avoid statements like the following: "The Strand Industries Main Plant receiving inspection did not reject any more shipments.")

Are the timing, frequency, and % defective consistent with the stated root cause?

We would expect to see the customer data in the Paynter chart as a part of the verification, but it should only supplement other data (i.e.: see above DO NOT rely on your customer for verification)

#5/6b. EXAMPLE – IMPLEMENT AND VERIFY PERMANENT CORRECTIVE ACTIONS

VERIFICATION OF CORRECTIVE ACTIONS

Paynter Chart
Showing Percent Defective (Rust) by Date with Pareto Chart

	D A T E					
Location	3/5	3/12	3/19	3/26	4/2	4/9
FAB HT	N/A	41%	21%	0%	0%	0%
Strand Ind.	0%	1.2%	3.7%	0%	0%	0%

Note: Containment actions implemented 3/22/13

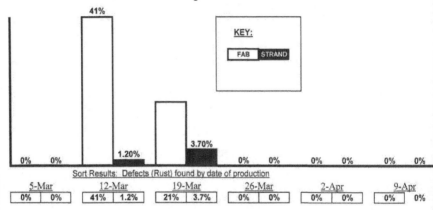

Note: Containment actions implemented 3/22/13

#5/6b COMMENTS

A Paynter chart is an effective display of data for the purpose of convincing your customer that containment and permanent corrective actions have been implemented. A Paynter Chart is simply a run chart with a Pareto Chart.

To illustrate a few actions directed toward root cause, consider an additional example in which the defect is breakage of plastic snap tabs on a plastic part determined to be the result of excessive stress.

Potential actions directed toward the true root cause:

Eliminate the Root Cause (i.e.: "tabs break" – redesign to eliminate stress by moving the tabs to other areas

Do an "end run" on the root cause. (i.e.: Eliminate tabs)

Design for robustness (i.e.: make tabs bigger, stronger, better stress loading, compliance, etc)

Actions toward the System Root Cause:

Update the DV plan to find this condition when it is under development.

Update the process sheets to include a check for broken tabs

Revise the DVP&R to include a requirement for tab robustness.

Other considerations:

Once actions are recommended ask the team the following questions:

Do these actions make sense when reviewing the root causes listed in section #4?

Do these actions adequately cover the location, timing, and magnitude as listed in the problem statement?

#7 EXAMPLE - PREVENT RECURRENCE

3/20/13 – The PFMEA was revised to add
RUST as a concern with the following
RPN Weights

SEVERITY =   6
DETECTION =   5
OCCURRENCE =   5   .
RPN = 150 (6x5x5)

As noted above, permanent preventive actions were implemented on
each of the process and system root causes.

#7 C O M M E N T S

Be sure to explore all necessary modifications to management and operating systems

Also consider all necessary modifications to practices and procedures.

The actions must be directed toward the Root Cause(s)

IMPORTANT – THE FOLLOWING ITEMS ARE NOT ALLOWED AS PREVENTIVE ACTIONS:

Detection Actions

Audits

Inspections

#8. EXAMPLE - RECOGNIZE THE TEAM

This could be anything from a short note of closure to a formal note in someone's personnel file recognizing both the individual's contribution and the spirit of the team approach.

For people outside of your immediate organization, this could be a business luncheon or if the contribution was "above and beyond," it could be notes to people's immediate supervisors.

#8 C O M M E N T S

Recognize the team effort.

Recognize the individual contributions

Document the efforts

Add the lessons learned to the organization knowledge base
  Significant/Critical Characteristics
PFMEA
  Process Sheets
  Design Guides
  FMEA
  Other…

Report to Management

Appendix I – Fishbone Diagram Example

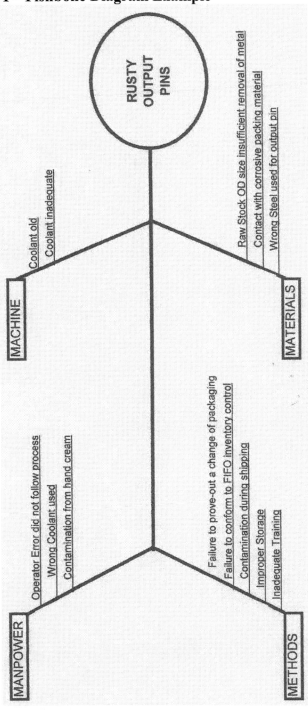

MACHINE
- Coolant old
- Coolant inadequate

MATERIALS
- Raw Stock OD size insufficient removal of metal
- Contact with corrosive packing material
- Wrong Steel used for output pin

RUSTY OUTPUT PINS

MANPOWER
- Operator Error did not follow process
- Wrong Coolant used
- Contamination from hand cream

METHODS
- Failure to prove-out a change of packaging
- Failure to conform to FIFO inventory control
- Contamination during shipping
- Improper Storage
- Inadequate Training

Appendix I – Comments on the Fishbone Diagram Example

The following illustration depicts the output of a team brainstorming effort as described in the section titled "#4a – DEFINE & VERIFY ROOT CAUSE.

As early as possible after team formation, the team leader should conduct a brainstorming session. During the brainstorming, the team leader presents an empty diagram with the problem in the circle and the "4M's" are already in the diagram: Manpower, Machine, Methods, and Materials. As an option, the team leader can suggest other general areas to include in the boxed areas of this diagram. Other areas such as Environment etc. could be added if the team felt it were necessary to facilitate brainstorming.

This session usually takes 1 to 2 hours to complete. It is most effective when knowledgeable people from all departments and areas which could have input in either correcting or verifying the problem under review. It is mandatory that group leader establish a relaxed climate free of fear of speaking out. The two most important rules are (1) Everyone contributes, even if it is a verbal "I don't know." and (2) No criticism. While it is ok to challenge input if you have added knowledge, but do not allow personal attacks or general negative statements.

All ideas should be put on the Fishbone diagram. After development of the Fishbone Diagram, the next step is to prioritize these POTENTIAL root causes.

Appendix II – Is/Is-Not Analysis

Rusty Output Pin		
IS	IS NOT	MAY BE
First observed 3/17/13 by Customer	Observed before 3/17/13	May have existed undetected in past
12% defective	100% defective	Other defect rates
	Found in Main Plant	Due to storage or transit
	Not a raw material issue	Packaging (new cardboard)
		Stock ID size (insufficient metal removal)
		Coolants - insufficient rust inhibitor

Appendix II – Comments on the Is/Is-Not Analysis

This is an optional exercise and it can be extremely useful. This is usually prepared by 1 or 2 individuals who have the most knowledge of the specific issue being investigated.

The Is/Is-Not Analysis should be completed before the brainstorming session and either displayed for the team to see or else given to team members as a handout.

The first 5-10 minutes of the brainstorming session should be devoted to a review and revision of the Is/Is-not analysis when all the team members can give their inputs.

Appendix III – Timeline

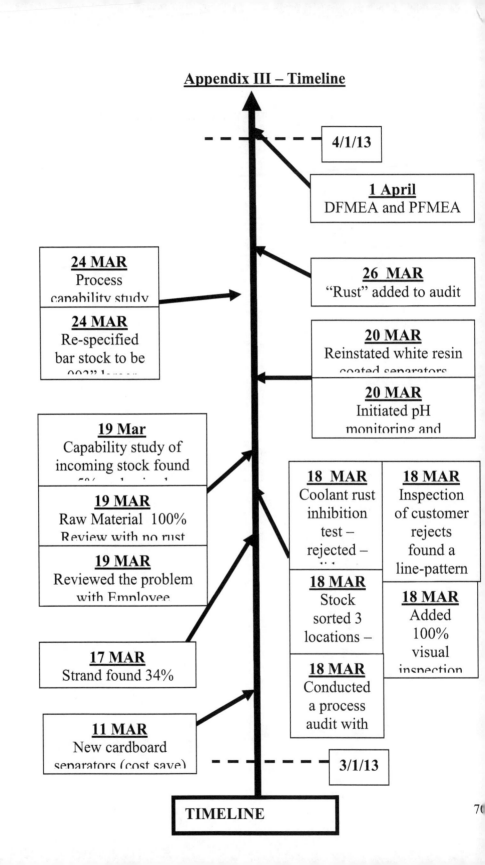

4/1/13

1 April
DFMEA and PFMEA

24 MAR
Process
capability study

26 MAR
"Rust" added to audit

24 MAR
Re-specified
bar stock to be
003" larger

20 MAR
Reinstated white resin
coated separators

20 MAR
Initiated pH
monitoring and

19 Mar
Capability study of
incoming stock found
5% declined

18 MAR
Coolant rust
inhibition
test –
rejected –

18 MAR
Inspection
of customer
rejects
found a
line-pattern

19 MAR
Raw Material 100%
Review with no rust

19 MAR
Reviewed the problem
with Employee

18 MAR
Stock
sorted 3
locations –

18 MAR
Added
100%
visual
inspection

17 MAR
Strand found 34%

18 MAR
Conducted
a process
audit with

11 MAR
New cardboard
separators (cost save)

3/1/13

TIMELINE

70

Appendix III– Comments on the Timeline

Similar to the Is/Is-Not Analysis, the Timeline analysis can also be extremely useful, especially for complicated issues.

 Again, this is usually prepared by 1 or 2 individuals who have the most knowledge of the specific issue being investigated.

Also, the Timeline should either be displayed or handed to the team members on a printed form. The review and revision of the Timeline should be conducted at the same time as the review of the Is/Is-Not analysis.

Authors Notes for *"8D Team Based Problem Solving"*

How many times should we ask WHY?

In reality, the quest for "why" should stop when it gets to things totally out of anyone's control. For an oversimplified example, consider that we were working on the problem of "The picture fell from the wall hanger." If we asked "Why?" until we got down to GRAVITY, we are obviously wasting our time. This seems trivial, but there are many environmental factors which, if listed as root cause, which is out of our control and would not lead to a solution. Typically, we protect from such a cause rather than fix them. For example:

> *We buy a picture hanger rated for this specific picture*
>
> *We make sure the wall is correct for the picture hanger*
>
> *We make sure the picture hanger is installed correctly*

The importance of a team effort

This can not be emphasized enough. It has been proven repeatedly that when people solve problems, the best individual effort is not as good as the worst effort by a proper team.

Formation of the team

The comments in section I (Use the Team Approach) cover this. However, here are some reinforcements that should be made.

Make a special effort to include people who <u>want</u> to work on the problem. Avoid those few people in the organization who are chronic complainers or otherwise have demonstrated an agenda not consistent with working within a team.

Who are the "Customers" in this issue?

Recognize that there are customers and suppliers within each organization. The Receiving Department is a Customer of both the supplier and the logistics firm. Additionally, the Receiving Department is a supplier to the Manufacturing Floor. The Manufacturing floor is a supplier to the Shipping Department. This reciprocal relationship takes place within all organizations.

Guard against "Groupthink."

This is a phenomenon in which individuals feel the organizational pressure to an extent they are more focused on trying to please the boss or otherwise insecure about the political ramifications of saying what they think. Some organizations with powerful leaders who tend to be "Top-down" type of managers make sure that such people are excluded from the team. In this case, it would be a good idea to begin the meeting by talking about groupthink as a possible detriment. Everyone should be made to feel comfortable in expressing their ideas. This is more important when some people see flaws in the system or product but have been rebuked by their co-workers, supervisors, or managers when they try to discuss these issues.

Be a Bulldog on containment
One of the most common causes of a repeat problem is failure to contain. Everyone can easily see the obvious areas to perform containment:

> *The manufacturing operation*

> *The customer's Receiving Dock*

> *The customer's Manufacturing Floor*

There are, however many other considerations which could contain product which should be evaluated:

> *Stock which has been put on hold for other considerations*

> *Stock which is within a rework or repair process (Separate from the direct manufacturing operation)*

Parts in shipment

Parts stored in distribution centers or warehouses, especially when these locations are at a remote location.

Customer returns for this reason or other reasons. (The "other reason" category is especially dangerous and must be evaluated).

"Show and Tell" parts which have been used for meetings, discussions or other illustrative purposes.

* * * * * * * * * * * * * * * *

Appendix B
Author's notes
for
"Team Oriented Problem Solving Part 2"

During my career within the automotive industry, I had the good fortune to spend significant time in many areas. These included Quality, Manufacturing, Engineering, Supplier Quality, Chemical and Metallurgical, and Total Quality Cost Management. This experience afforded me a unique insight into the way problems were handled. I was able to receive mentorship from some of the best minds the industry had to offer. This mentorship gently nudged me when I tried to set a course which was in one way or another dysfunctional. I became a team leader for many problem solving groups with a successful track record. As a result, I have a distinct feeling for what works and what does not.

This book is an attempt to give the reader the benefit of this experience which was collected over more than 40 years. Whether the reader is a current or future facilitator or an active participant in group problem solving, I am offering one person's view of the path to success in problem solving.

Below, I give my contact information and if anyone wishes to discuss their particular problem solving effort, I would be glad to provide comments accordingly.

Regards,

Marc Possley

****

I hope you will find this book helpful in improving the problem solving efforts within your organization. If you have recommendations for corrections or otherwise to improve this book, please let me know. mcpoz@comcast.net

Made in the USA
Columbia, SC
16 October 2020